EVERYTHING IS ENERGY
ENERGY IS EVERYTHING

Mia Wise

BALBOA.
PRESS

Balboa Press books may be ordered through booksellers or by contacting:

Balboa Press
A Division of Hay House
1663 Liberty Drive
Bloomington, IN 47403
www.balboapress.com
1-(877) 407-4847

Because of the dynamic nature of the Internet, any Web addresses or
links contained in this book may have changed since publication and
may no longer be valid. The views expressed in this work are solely those
of the author and do not necessarily reflect the views of the publisher,
and the publisher hereby disclaims any responsibility for them.

The author of this book does not dispense medical advice or prescribe the use
of any technique as a form of treatment for physical, emotional, or medical
problems without the advice of a physician, either directly or indirectly. The
intent of the author is only to offer information of a general nature to help
you in your quest for emotional and spiritual well-being. In the event you use
any of the information in this book for yourself, which is your constitutional
right, the author and the publisher assume no responsibility for your actions.

Any people depicted in stock imagery provided by Thinkstock are models,
and such images are being used for illustrative purposes only.
Certain stock imagery © Thinkstock.

ISBN: 978-1-4525-0074-4 (sc)
ISBN: 978-1-4525-0075-1 (e)

Printed in the United States of America

Balboa Press rev. date: 11/16/2010

Since everything is …
Energy

We need to know
how to be …

The right energy

Our happiness depends

on it

Our success depends

on it

Our health depends

on it

and ... even other people

depend on it

This divine spark

It's how we came into
existence…

essentially, how everything
came to be…

from this thing called…
energy

You know how you can
just feel someones'
sadness?

Or anger? Or happiness?

That's energy

It can't be seen
can't be touched

Yet it leaves evidence
behind for sensitives
to perceive

Energy lives on long after
An event has happened

We shape our thoughts

We shape our bodies

We shape the events
In our week

When was the last time
you took time
to shape … your energy?

Like brushing our teeth …

Eating 3 squares …

Getting some sleep …

Don't we need to :

Clean,
Feed,
Nurture,

our energy?

Everything we do requires it.

Everything we think is sparked by it.

Everything we say is preceded by it.

And at the end of the day
We retire it without regard
Or care

If you have the wrong energy …
You'll know it

If you converse with another
And you feel them pull away …

They may be in a rush or …
preoccupied

Or … you just might have
" wrong energy"

If you aren't invited places

Or the room goes silent

when you walk in

If people are always too busy

to do anything with you …

You've got wrong energy

If people don't genuinely smile to see you …
Drop what they're doing to chat for a few …
Or make silly excuses to break a …
date

They could be feeling tired. Or ill.

Or … it could be that you have real wrong energy

Maybe some or none of these things happen to you …
Maybe not yet …
Maybe not ever

Maybe you'd like just to purify,
Strengthen the energy you already have

Maybe you'd like to enjoy happier connections …

Have friends,

family …

Even strangers – love being

around you …

anytime

Maybe you'd like others to seek you out …

have the job offers,

favors,

gifts,

attention …

come your way

Be treated like a … Queen

or … a King

If so, it all begins and ends …
with your energy

There is right energy
There is wrong energy
There is good energy
There is bad energy

There is high energy
There is low energy

There is strong energy
There is weak energy

Sometimes, even no energy

To make good energy –
Learn to be calm

Love silence. Love quiet things.
Sit by a tree in a quiet place.
Speak to God and ask Him to speak back.

Vow to clear all dark, ugly
thoughts …
Ask Him to cleanse you

Widen your inner world
expand your self ... less ... ness

So that when you're in the
presence of others ...
you can ...

Focus on radiating
strong,
loving
energy

Nothing else empowers you more

When someone speaks to you,
listen with patience and interest

if you listen with your heart –
you will hear their soul

Stomp on your ego and keep it from
planning what next to say
to top the others' story

Let your heart open ... to ...
rejoice
sympathize
synchronize
empathize

Energy Bath

Take one … Give one

Close your eyes …

See everything inside as a blank white screen.

Hold it. Hold it. Hold it.

Open your eyes …

Now give that essence to whomever you encounter

Let others acclimate to you
before rushing them

For instance; when a person just comes home or …
walks into a room –
allow the energies to blend and warm first,
before firing a barrage of questions,
or shouting the events of the day

People are receptive only when their energies are

Clean your energy daily

Remember the powerful life force it is

Don't poison it or kill it with ugly thoughts and feelings

Clean and calm your energy daily

All your successes big and small depend on it

The thing about energy is that …
it is working for you
all the time

It works for you
or it works
against you

Your choice.

When you break down any relationship you value …

what is it exactly

you value?

Isn't it about the way it makes you feel?

There you go. The energy.

It's the energy.

No matter who it is, everyone can use a bit of …
"good energy"
sent their way

Radiating clear, clean
vibrations
uplifts the other …
and heals yourself

ENERGY is EVERYTHING
EVERYTHING is ENERGY

It is
the fuel God gave us when we were born
and the fuel He gives us to run on throughout our lives

But it's up to us to make it good …
Or bad

One type makes life go smoother,
The other flatlines

The type of energy you have makes or breaks you.

Good energy is clean, positive …
life giving.
It's magnetic.

Bad energy is polluted, negative,
life taking –
repelling

Cultivate your energy
as though your life depends upon it
because it does

You will only be as successful
as your energy is
pure

It's fine and good to work on your physique,

get in shape,

stay toned

Just make sure you're not merely a …

beautifully wrapped present …

with nothing inside

People will usually perceive
the real intent behind
your words

Why?

Oh because energy speaks louder than words

While in the presence of others
Shut down the logical,
analytical,
human
mind

In place of judgements, begrudgements …
just be peace

Like the serenely flowing
stream
quietly
meandering

Your energy is your most prized possession

It's more important and more impacting
than the status you hold …

the possessions you own …

or the money you make

Guard it like gold for in the end
when all is said and done
you'll only be remembered for …
the energy you were

All is about energy

How people regard you

Why events happen

When you have energy filled with

humility

calm

respect

Watch how everything begins …

to …

flow

Your body is the temple of God
Your energy is the essence
Everything in our life is affected by energy

How do you want to affect
lives?
How do you want your energy
to be?

Created by –
the energy of
Amelia Wise